SUCCESS THROUGH YOUR EYES

Learning from Your World to Find Your Way

Christina Wenman

Success Through Your Eyes: Learning from Your World to Find Your Way by Christina Wenman

Published by Christina Wenman

ISBN: 9780692064320

Printed in the United States of America

Contents

How to Get the Most Out of This Book

At the end of the chapters, I have "Think About It" questions that I encourage you to read through and answer. Answering or even simply thinking about these questions will help you get the most out of this book. You can write your answers down on a separate piece of paper or in the margins. Understand that these are questions that require deep thought, so feel free to take your time on them and answer them truthfully. Then, use the "Act on It" suggestions to make some real changes!

Introduction

Success is not one-dimensional. It is not elusive. It is not a single statement of achievement. No, this book is not about all that success isn't; nor is it about how to achieve it, but it is one that will provide a greater understanding of what it could mean for you. The reality of it is that the term "success" cannot be defined by one person for the rest to follow and use, it must be defined by each individual person to use for their own life. Yes, I am only a teenager, and I, in no way, have all the answers. This is why I set out to find them. I spent time interviewing people whom I consider to be successful, and

I have gained insight into how their ideas of a successful life have developed with their years of experience.

As a teenager, it can be tough to gain a vast amount of experience (not to be confused with knowledge) in what it means to have fulfilling success. Yes, earning straight A's and doing well in school can be considered a form of being successful, but does that mean that it will instantly fill the rest of our life with purpose and meaning? Probably not. Yes, it can boost confidence and increase short-term happiness, but in reality, straight A's do not sustain us. This lack of experience is what makes it so easy to classify success through one-dimensional things such as wealth, status, fame, or power.

There are so many books on how to achieve success, but without knowing what success really means to *you*, how do you expect to achieve it?

Imagine that there are three people: Jake, Katie, and John.

Jake's idea of success is power and being able to make the rules. His ideal vision of a successful life may entail being a governor, the CEO of a large company, or even the President of the United States.

Next is Katie. Her idea of success surrounds wealth. She wants to be able to buy anything that her heart desires, and she strives to have a job to meet her monetary standards. Katie may want to become a neurosurgeon, a doctor, or a lawyer. She isn't looking at these jobs because they are what she is really passionate about, but after doing research, she found that these jobs supposedly pay really well.

Last but not least, John's idea of success is being able to help others. Whether it be through charitable acts or simply being able to put a smile on others' faces, John feels successful by playing a part in others' happiness.

Now.

All three people go to the bookstore and see a book that claims to solve all of their problems. It guarantees them success as long as they read the book, learn the lessons, and follow what it tells them to do.

They all read the book.

Does Jake automatically become the President? Does Katie immediately become a billionaire? Does John instantly create an entire state of world peace? The answer is simply no. But why?

The books about how to become successful are incredibly helpful because they teach you valuable skills and mindsets that are crucial in the function of a successful mind. Although, just simply having the "valuable skills and mindsets that are crucial in the function of a successful mind" does not automatically guarantee that you will become the President, become a neurosurgeon, or even create world peace.

You need to understand what your goals are and what success means to you. You then apply the skills and mindsets to achieve your goals and become your version of "successful."

You cannot fully rely on one way to become successful. The road to success is not one single path, as a matter of fact, no two people can use the same road to get there.

Well, what is success then? Below is a list I put together of several definitions created by different sources.

Success is...

"The favorable or prosperous termination of attempts or endeavors; the accomplishment of one's goals." (Dictionary.com)

"Having the courage, the determination, and the will to become the person you believe you were meant to be." (George Sheehan)

"The accomplishment of an aim or purpose." (Oxford Dictionary)

"Put your heart, mind, intellect, and soul into even your smallest acts. This is the secret of success." (Swami Sivananda)

"Success isn't about how much money you make; it's about the difference you make in people's lives." (Michelle Obama)

"Liking yourself, liking what you do, and liking how you do it." (Maya Angelou)

"Clarity of my intention and reaching that intention while being true to myself and with joy." (India Arie)

"Success is the ability to go from one failure to another with no loss of enthusiasm." (Winston Churchill)

"Being wealthy in wisdom, abundant in appreciation, rich in relationships, prosperous in purpose, comfortable with yourself...oh, and having some money, too. If you've got 5 out of the 6, you are way more successful than any person who only has the last." (Doe Zantamata)

"Success isn't something that just happens - success is learned, success is practiced, and then it is shared." (Sparky Anderson)

"Being able to go to sleep and feel good about myself, and about my life and the people around me." (Agapi Stassinopoulos)

"Success means being able to wake up every morning and do the things you love. It means feeling awake, alive, and connected to what has meaning and purpose in your life. It means being able to touch and engage with those you love, your family, your friends. And it means being in a state of vibrant, awake, alive health." (Dr. Mark Hyman)

"A third measure of success that goes beyond the two metrics of money and power, and consists of four pillars: well-being, wisdom, wonder, and giving." (Arianna Huffington)

"Success is peace of mind, which is a direct result of self-satisfaction in knowing you did your best to become the best you are capable of becoming." (John Wooden)

"The more you're actively and practically engaged, the more successful you will feel." (Richard Branson)

"Success in life could be defined as the continued expansion of happiness and the progressive realization of worthy goals." (Deepak Chopra)

"Success is 1% inspiration, 99% perspiration." (Thomas Edison)

"Success is 99% attitude and 1% aptitude." (Celestine Chua)

"Success is not counted by how high you have climbed, but by how many people you have brought with you." (Wil Ros)

"Success is dependent on effort." (Sophocles)

"Success is the sum of small efforts, repeated day in and day out." (Robert Collier)

When I talk about success in this book, I am not talking about a literal definition of success; that cannot be changed. Instead, I am talking about what you consider a successful life to be, past simply accomplishing your goals and getting what you need or want. While these are all accurate definitions, they are not 100% yours. If you have not already created your personal definition of success, I encourage you to look through these definitions and use them as ideas to help you formulate your own - because your definition is the only one that matters!

Think About It

Which of the definitions provided is your favorite?

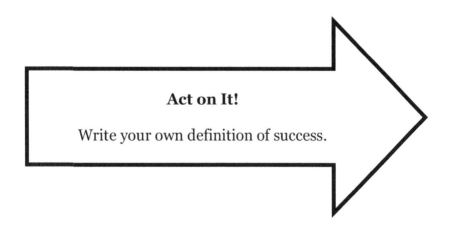

Act on It!

Write your own definition of success.

Part 1

Who ARE You?

1

What Do You Do?

Picture this scene – you're at a family holiday party when your extended relatives ask the question you've been dreading: What do you do? Other forms of this question include: What is your major? What is your job? Where do you go or want to go to school? What are your plans after school? The problem with these questions is that whatever you say can immediately determine what that person thinks about you and will direct how the rest of the conversation will go. Depending on what you say, you can be put into a certain stereotype in their perspective, which typically does not fully align with exactly who you are - and most likely not how you want to be known.

Isn't it interesting that we visualize certain careers on an up & down "successful" scale? When we determine a person's significance by their career, we tend to see past who they are as a person and how they want to be known. It is also interesting to understand the difference between the average salary for a specific career and what a person actually makes in that career. For example, the salary range for a business owner could easily be anywhere from less than $50,000 to more than $5 billion - of course, it depends on the company and the person's involvement in the company. The same goes for any other profession.

Don't let what you do be the only thing that defines who you are. We need to stop asking the overused questions that request one sentence answers. We must start asking questions that require real thought and inspire conversations. This is how we start to get to know people by their own definition - and not by one that we mindlessly make up of them. It is not your responsibility to say what drives another person; it IS your responsibility to find out what drives you and share it with others.

As I mentioned before, I am not talking about the technical definition of winning or achieving something; I am talking about success on a deeper and all-encompassing level - having a successful and fulfilling life. It is not your career that measures your success. However, it is *why* you are in your career and who you are in everything that you choose to do that can help you find purpose; inevitably determining whether you feel successful or not.

Some people, especially teenagers, dislike the question "why?" because it forces us to think on a deeper level. Although, without asking questions that require thought, what is the purpose of asking questions in the first place? If we spend our whole lives asking only questions that we could easily find the answer to on our smartphone in a couple clicks, we slowly start thinking less and less. The less we think, the harder it is to find our purpose.

Act on It!

Complete a personality assessment and/or an interest inventory.

Make a list of your greatest strengths.

2

Defining YOU

Imagine you are laying in your casket at your funeral while the eulogy is being read. No, really, think about it. People are given the opportunity to say a few words about you. Who is the first to step forward? Is it a friend or family member? What are they saying? Now ask yourself: what do you *want* people to say about you? Perhaps that you were generous and caring to everyone around you, or that your personality always brightened up the room, or that you were able to think about the world with a unique perspective. What type of person do you want to be? Which specific qualities or traits do you want to have and maintain? Which qualities or traits do you want to change? Chances are, you probably know the answer to these questions, but the ultimate question then becomes: are you living your life in a way that leads you to be the person you wish to become? If the answer is no, then why not?

I have noticed that when we are younger, we tend to see success as though it is on one scale; one person is either more or less successful than the next. What I have learned through this process is that, typically, as individuals grow older, they slowly stop focusing so much on other people, and start to focus more on what is relevant to their own aspirations.

You know how you aren't supposed to compare apples to oranges? It's the same thing when it comes to the topic of success. If you're doing it right, your definition of success should be completely original and different from the people around you. Therefore, you shouldn't be able to compare your life to others and say that one person is any more successful than the next.

Sometimes it can be easy to put people on a scale depending on their job. I have noticed that the more experienced people get, the more likely they are to understand that it becomes less of an up & down scale, and more of a neutral spectrum when it comes to careers and success.

When it comes to school, this scale looks pretty similar. When we hear about if or where someone is going to college, we may look at how "prestigious" or "well-known" that college is, and because of that, we are likely to subconsciously conclude how smart the person is and how successful they will be in the future.

What I think is especially sad, is that sometimes we get so caught up in how "smart" people seem and how much money people make. When in reality, the SAT score and the amount of money in a person's wallet will *never* predict a person's character; nor their happiness; nor their success. Whatsoever.

It is what you put your thought and effort into everyday that will lead you directly to the person you become. It sounds obvious, but in reality, if everyone were to live their life and take action with this mindset, we would all be living in a completely different world. We would also begin to find our purpose in life and be able to express it to those around us.

Think About It

How do you want to be remembered?

Are you living your life in a way that leads you to be the person you wish to become?

When you are laying in your casket at your funeral while the eulogy is being read, what types of things do you want people to say about you?

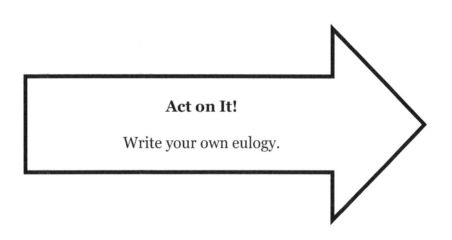

Act on It!

Write your own eulogy.

3

How Did We Get Here?

As a six-year-old, we all had different likes and dislikes. Some liked to draw with crayons, while others preferred to paint. Some liked learning about math, while others enjoyed reading more. For some, recess was their favorite time of the day, while others' favorite time of the day was lunchtime. These differences never created a barrier of judgement or snobbery. Everyone had their friend groups, but that was not solely determined by their interests or favorite times of the day.

Snob /snäb/ noun - a person who judges the importance of people mainly by their social position or wealth, and who believes social position or wealth makes one person better than others. (Cambridge English Dictionary)

Six years later and we began to figure out what our favorite classes were. For most kids, middle school wasn't the best because of how harshly students judge each other. We narrowed down our favorite classes and maybe started getting ideas about what we could be when we grow up, but they were never set in stone. Most of the judgement in middle school did not come from what you were good at and enjoyed doing for classes, but rather your appearance and superficial features.

Two years later, high school rolled around. This is when the new friendships began to form. Since there are four grades in high school, people tend to hang out with people who are older or younger than them. People like people who are like themselves; it's inevitable. The friendships form with the people who have similar interests. Not because the people who have other interests are "better or worse," but because you have more in common and can talk about the things you enjoy without one person getting annoyed or ignoring what the other has to say. For most high school students, knowing exactly how they want their future to go is not something that they want to think about. It creates stress and puts focus onto something that requires a lot of thought. As a high school student, it seems as though when you are planning or thinking about your life after school, it has to be perfect because if you change your mind too late, your future will be ruined. Although, as you get older you realize that is not the case, since you will probably change your mind, and that's okay.

Then senior year happens. The discovery of what you want to do really kicks into gear. College applications and scholarships can get overwhelming when you are trying to balance them with AP classes, clubs, sports, social life, work, etc. Even if you aren't sure that you want to go to college, you have to decide fast because deadlines come up quickly. Senior year is also when the "Christmas Party Questions" become a norm: "What is your job?" "Where do you go or want to go to school?" "What's your major?" "What are your plans after school?" These questions can become intimidating because they trap you into one expectation that you are going to college, which may force you to feel that you have to because it's the "normal" thing to do. While college is valuable because it helps you get a good education and provides you with novel experiences, it is not for everyone. The "Christmas Party Questions" can almost steer your life for you because they can make you feel that you have to go to college to get a "good" (normal) future. This is when the snobbery begins to sprout.

Another six years pass and you're at a holiday party with your friends; you don't know a lot of people there. This is where first impressions make or break you. The most commonly asked icebreaker is "What do you do?" Implying: "What is your job?" without directly assuming that you have a job. You answer this question and depending on what you say, the person may react either interested or fake interested. In their mind, they may even be putting you on a scale that determines your success. You talk about your job or "what you do" for a brief moment, and then you run out of things to talk about because all of the normal things to talk about have already been discussed. You part ways and repeat this same conversation with other people until the party's over. You look back on the night and realize that all you did was recite everything that anyone could have already found from your Facebook or LinkedIn profiles, and you learned the same about other people. What would happen if we were to stop asking "What do you do?" and start asking questions like "What motivates you?" "What do you love?" and "Why do you do what you do?"

Can you Imagine?

...if we started asking questions that require real thought and inspire conversations?

...if we started to get to know people by their own definition and not by the one we mindlessly makeup of them?

...if we took the responsibility to find out what drives us and share it with others?

...if we stopped asking the questions that require us to recite facts about ourselves, and start asking the questions that make us think and inspire others?

Think About It

What do you "do?" Would you want that to be the only thing people know about you?

What do you love?

Why do you do what you do?

Act on It!

Make a list of great questions you can ask when meeting someone new.

Part 2

My Mission to Find Answers

As a kid, I've noticed that people love to talk about this thing called "success." I have also noticed that people tend to look at "success" as though it is something that one person creates, which is then to be measured and discussed by others. I once had a conversation with one of my peers in 7th grade, let's call her Sarah, that began when I asked her if she knew what she wanted to do when she grows up. Her eyes lit up and she replied confidently "Yes, I want to be the CEO of a very large company." "Do you know what type of company?" I asked. She replied with "No, just a really big one." I then asked her why, and she said it was because CEOs supposedly make a lot of money. Not only was this generalizing all CEOs into one "billionaire" category, it also didn't seem as though she had actually ever taken time to think about all of the hard work, commitment, time, and persistence that you must have when you want to get to the top of a company.

Another more recent conversation I had was also about future career paths. I was talking to a friend of mine about what his plans were for college and he said, "I think I will probably go to the University of Wisconsin-Madison for business school or maybe medical school, I guess I'm not completely sure." He does well in high school and he was able to get accepted. I then asked him "Why? Those are two very different paths, you know." He replied "Well, I think either of those fields would lead me to a pretty good career." I then asked him what his dream job would be - what job he believes would give him the most satisfaction without any regard to money. He replied with "I mean if I am being completely honest, my dream job would probably be a history teacher because I would love going into work every day knowing that I have the power to positively impact kids' lives while teaching them about things that I'm passionate about." I was shocked that he said that, because a lot of times the reason people don't end up in their dream job is because it seems too far-fetched or elusive. He could easily go down the path to become a history teacher, his dream job, so why wouldn't he? He was worried about not earning enough money and the way his peers would view him.

When I ask other teenagers about their ideas of success, their initial responses tend to revolve around the ideas of money, belongings, recognition, fame, achieving specific goals, etc. Given that they are young, they tend to initially react with unsure blank stares, as the typical teenager doesn't look very deep into the topic of what it means to have a successful life. I notice that the younger people are, the more they tend to focus their idea of success on what *society* considers to be successful.

In our world today, there is a lot of judgement. It is our culture to talk regularly about how much money other people make, what other people do, and how successful or unsuccessful other people are. Because we know that whatever we do will be critiqued by others, it can be easy to fall into the trap of fixing your life with the main goal of impressing others. We think about which jobs will get us the most money, so we can buy the biggest house, and everyone can talk about how successful we are. Even though there is a lot of focus on these superficial things, in reality, the people who you are trying to impress don't genuinely care as much as their judgement makes it seem - and if for some reason they actually do, are they even the type of people who you would want to impress anyways? Hopefully not.

When others know how much money you make, they fall into one of three different categories:

1. The people who make more money than you.
2. The people who make the same amount of money as you.
3. The people who make less money than you.

The people who make more money than you will not care how much you make.

The people who make the same amount of money as you will feel neutral or possibly feel the need to make more than you.

The people who make less money than you may not believe you.

It sounds like a lose-lose-lose situation to me.

So here comes the question: What is more important to you - being able to constantly impress others who don't *actually* care or feeling satisfied coming into work every day knowing that you are making an impact by doing what you love? I am in no way saying that having a job that pays a lot of money is not the kind of job that you should seek out, nor am I saying that having a big house or an expensive car is bad. What you choose to do with the money you make is a very personal choice. Whatever you choose to do, choose it with thought and do it for yourself, and not for the purpose of "impressing" others.

I wanted to get a better understanding of how "successful" people view success and how their perceptions have developed since they were younger, so I sought out people whom I consider to be successful and asked them these ten questions.

1. How would you define success today compared to when you were younger?
2. What are the key attributes that helped you get to where you are today?
3. Who helped you the most along the way? Did you have any specific mentors or teachers who made an impact? What did you learn from them?
4. What is the best piece of advice you have ever gotten?
5. What is your favorite book?
6. If you could go back in time, what would you want to tell your teenage self?
7. If you could change one thing in the world, what would it be?
8. Do you consider yourself to be an introvert or an extrovert?
9. What was the one thing that impacted you the most?
10. What was the biggest mistake you have ever made and/or if you could do anything differently, what would it be?

"Just going through this process is forcing me to think about things that I wouldn't have thought about before - which in essence is teaching me something about myself - therefore, I am learning from a 17-year-old girl." - Jay Forte, Speaker, Certified Coach, Author of <u>The Greatness Zone</u>, and Owner of "The Forte Factor, LLC"

When I heard Jay Forte say this to me, it really helped me open my eyes and realize that you learn from everyone who you come into contact with - not just "mentors." It was exciting to know that I was able to make an impact on the people I was interviewing as well.

As I completed the interviews, I noticed that although the perspectives of the people varied, there were three key points that continually surfaced. I have created the next three chapters to share with you the most important things I learned from the diverse group of people I interviewed.

Think About It

Who are your mentors?

Who do you think is learning from you?

Do you think that you are creating your goals for yourself or to sound "good" to other people?

Act on It!
Create your own list of questions you would like to ask people you consider to be successful.

Choose three people you would like to interview and interview them!

4

Continuous Learning

If you are someone in school who is reading this now, you may be thinking something like "I can't wait to get out of school, when I won't have to study, do homework, take tests, and learn anymore." You may tend to let the words "homework," "studying," and "tests" become interchangeable with the term "learning" (as they are used to explain the dread of school). Once school is done, all of those things will be over, right?

Wrong.

Yes, school will be done, and you will not have the required classes and homework every day, but you will still be learning throughout every aspect of your life, whether you want to or not. Learning is something that can be done through many different channels and not solely by taking classes. As you grow up, you realize that you can learn a great deal from reading books, watching videos, seeking out mentors, and even simply incorporating listening and noticing into your everyday life. Having the willingness to listen will allow you to open up your eyes to a vast amount of opportunities and knowledge.

"Continuous learning is something that you have to embrace and take seriously. Be a continuous learner."

- Rich Poirier, CEO, Church Mutual Insurance Company

A common misconception is that you can only learn from people who have reached a higher level than you. This is one of the most self-limiting thoughts that a person could have. If you lived your whole life without realizing that you can learn from everyone, think about the opportunities you would miss!

I had the opportunity to interview Bart Starr Jr. in a small cafe in Birmingham, Alabama. I learned a lot from him, but there was one thing he talked about that really stood out. He said that it is important to always remember that you can learn just as much from the person pumping gas next to you than you can from a mentor.

"My dad has always taught me to treat everybody with the same level respect, no matter his or her title, regardless of their rank, or what they have accomplished in business."
- Bart Starr Jr., Investment Broker and son of Hall of Fame Quarterback, Bart Starr

It is amazing what you are able to learn when you start to incorporate this idea of noticing and listening into your day-to-day life.

"What a shame it would be if individuals didn't realize that right there in front of you, at a place you would go regularly, could be somebody who you actually find to be inspiring. It would be a real missed opportunity to go into a place like that and not realize that right there you might meet somebody who could change your life for the better. Think it has to be somebody famous or well-known? Not at all." - Bart Starr Jr.

Do not underestimate the power of a strong mentor who is willing share their wisdom with you. However, once you open up and take every encounter and discussion (from everyone) as a learning opportunity, you can gain wisdom no matter where you are in your life, and your growth would be immeasurable.

With learning comes listening; with listening comes learning.

"Listening is a skill that I have to continuously hone, and it is underappreciated."

- Rich Poirier

Listening is a skill that is extremely underrated, and once you are able to hone this skill, your ability to learn from the people around you will grow tremendously. We have all heard it before: hearing and listening are two separate things. When we are talking, we are not listening. We can *hear* and talk at the same time, but we cannot *listen* and talk at the same time. Listening is not a matter of just using your ears; listening requires giving someone our full attention. Sometimes we get too caught up in what we want to share, and we forget to realize that another person's perspective may be even more valuable than ours.

Simon Sinek said in one of his popular talks, "If you agree with somebody, don't nod yes. If you disagree with somebody, don't nod no." At first, this seems like an unorthodox approach to listening, but once you understand why he says what he says, it begins to become more clear. When you listen, don't just listen to figure out what the person is saying, but instead listen with the intent to learn and comprehend *why* they are saying what they're saying. Anyone can have the same view as you, but not everyone with the same view has the same reasoning to why they believe what they believe.

Perhaps there is a controversial election with two candidates. You can either vote for candidate A or candidate B. You voted for candidate B and have your reasons for doing so. Your friend voted for the same person, but is their reason the same as yours? Maybe or maybe not. Just because they vote for the same person does not automatically mean that their political view is identical to yours.

Your reasons for voting for candidate B are obviously different from why someone else may have chosen candidate A, and your reasons for voting for candidate B could have easily been different than someone else who voted the same way. It is important to listen to people who both agree and disagree with us because we can learn from understanding their perspective.

Stop and Notice

"In the morning when I came down the stairs for breakfast, my father made us look around, stop, and notice something each day."
- Jay Forte

I found this exercise, suggested by Jay Forte, to be especially interesting because once we begin to notice the things around us and stop living our lives on auto-pilot, we are able to clearly find more value in things, people, and experiences.

Do you ever get that feeling when you go through your whole day and then later realize that you don't remember even doing half of the things you did? Or when you are driving and get to your destination; you look around and realize that you don't remember any of the drive? Typically, when you first get your license, this doesn't happen because everything is so new to you, but as you get more familiar with everything, you go through what feels like the same motions, and you see what seems like the same scenery. It isn't until we begin to stop and notice that we are able to slow down our lives and find new and more valuable aspects of something that we are already familiar with. There was one day in particular I decided that I was going to start "noticing" things on my ride home. I was on my way home from school and I was looking around. I vividly remember seeing: the most beautiful sunset, the leaves turning bright colors, a tractor in the field, etc. If I wouldn't have actively decided to notice, it would've been just like any other day, and I would have driven home only to realize that I didn't remember any of the drive. All from that one drive home, I started to gain a greater appreciation for all of the simple things that surround us every day.

I think it's sad that so many people tie the idea of learning directly to school. It sounds weird to think that learning and school shouldn't be so closely related, but the way that some school systems are set up makes it difficult for kids to *want* to learn.

When I was in middle school, I dreaded going to school every day because I was scared to make mistakes and get into trouble. At our school, we had disciplinary action forms which had to be taken home and signed by parents. They were called "pink slips," and they were given out if you did something that was not safe, trustworthy, respectful, or responsible.

The problem with "pink slips" was that something as innocent as forgetting to get your planner signed off by your parents was treated with the same level of punishment as bullying someone on the playground. Another problem was that it showed us middle school kids that we should be ashamed to make even the smallest of mistakes. I understand the reasoning behind being disciplined for saying something mean to another student, but for accidentally forgetting your scissors in your locker? Come on.

For me, it was the fear of making mistakes, but there are so many other reasons that some people relate school to negative experiences. For others, it may be test anxiety, loads of homework, getting up in the morning, pressure to get perfect grades, or bullies. Whatever it is, it's really sad to see kids getting steered away from learning by an establishment that is created for that exact purpose. If you are currently in school and you despise learning because of the deep dread that comes with the homework, forced studying and memorization, bullies, or anxiety, I challenge you to look at learning from a different perspective and begin to enjoy learning for what it really is. Learning does not stop when school stops - and that is a good thing.

"I believe that it is necessary to always be honing one's craft, improving one's skill set, sharpening one's sword, and being a lifelong learner." - Kevin Hermening, Marine Veteran and Certified Financial Planner

Do you remember the stage that every little kid goes through when they question everything? It all starts when they ask one simple "why" question that has no definite answer. You answer it to the best of your ability, and they directly come back with "why?" You get struck with what seems to be a thousand why's - most of which you do not know the answer to. My question is: when does that *why* stage stop? At what point does it become normal to not ask questions? At what point are we supposed to stop questioning the world? Are we just supposed to lose that strong desire to understand?

When we are born, everything is new to us and nothing makes sense. We use all of our senses to figure things out. If someone gives us a cup, we try to understand by feeling it, tasting it, looking at it, and in some cases, banging it to hear what noise it makes. We get a little bit older and things start to become more normal to us. We learn that a cup is used to drink from, and we learn not to question it. Once we are old enough, if someone puts a cup in front of us, we think "it's a cup, you drink from it." Obviously - but we stop questioning it. Why?

"Stay humble and realize that there is a lot of wisdom out there. There are a lot of good role models and good teachers that you can find if you are willing to do so. Have the willingness to listen." - *Bart Starr Jr.*

Act on It!

Set aside a specific time each week to learn
something new!

5

Authenticity

"Success is about self-expression and becoming who you are. Success is being who you want to be, doing what you want to do, and going where you want to go." - Daniel Ally, International Business Expert and 3-time Best Selling Author

Most can agree with the simple fact that everyone in the world is different. We are born into *different* environments, have *different* perspectives on life, get motivated by *different* things, react *differently* in certain scenarios, have *different* strengths and weaknesses, etc. Now you're probably getting sick of this word due to semantic satiation, but it's the word that we all need to hear and comprehend. *Different.*

We have to understand that even though we can be similar to another person and have a lot of things in common, there will always be something that sets you apart from the next. You're *different*. This is exactly why you have to create your own definition of success, your own steps, and your own life because if you follow someone else's steps to having a fulfilling and successful life, you will never be 100% satisfied. Because it is not 100% *you*.

"Stop conforming, start performing."

- Daniel Ally

Wouldn't it be a lot easier if there was simply a key to life that would just tell you which decisions to make in order to be successful? The only problem with that is if everyone followed one key to life, everyone would end up in the same place and nobody would be happy. The world needs "different" to survive. We need people who are willing to do the things that we are not willing to do, and vice versa. Take two completely different jobs: A park ranger and a lawyer. Typically, someone who is a park ranger would not think about ever becoming a lawyer. Chances are, there are some careers that you would never want to have, and the people in those jobs wouldn't want to have yours, but either way, the world needs both!

What people tend to find out as they grow up is this: Life's purpose isn't to only make the "right" choice and live without flaws, rather it is to fail, go through different experiences, learn, and reflect on them. In all seriousness, I believe that "life's purpose" is for people in life to find their own purpose.

Imagine you listened to the advice someone gave you in order to be successful and followed exactly what they said to do. Congratulations, you did the exact same thing that another person did and you lived the same way! Given that the outcomes would still be slightly different due to the unique opportunities, environments, and time frames, what satisfaction would that give you? You can't reach self-actualization by following other people. It's in the name: SELF-actualization. If we were supposed to all reach that level of satisfaction the same way, perhaps it would simply be called actualization.

"Success is what you make it. It's a self-determined thing... not tangible, not comparable... just your own measurements."
- *Tyrone M. Robinson III, Speaker, Owner of "Opportunities 2 Serve," and Author of* <u>*The Light Within Us All*</u>

Your idea of success in life should be meaningful to you and not formatted only to sound impressive to others. For example, if your goal is to become rich and famous, get a big house, and an expensive car for the sole purpose of impressing others, what is your goal really worth to you? The goals that you create for yourself are the goals that are more likely to get accomplished, and once they get accomplished, they ultimately give you more satisfaction.

It is not only about *what* your goal is, but it is also about *why* your goal is what it is. Whenever you set a goal for yourself, big or small, ask yourself *why* you have created that goal. Sometimes we tend to focus so much on the *what*, even when the *why* is more important.

We will take the example from before; perhaps your goal is to become a billionaire. Why is that your goal? Do you have a business that you want to start up? Do you wish to impress others with your money and status? Do you have a specific charity or research fund that you would want to help out? The list of answers to the question "why" continues...

James is a Senior in high school and his goal is to become a millionaire and have a big house with at least two sports cars. His goal was not created solely for himself, and his goal's main purpose was to impress the people around him. On June 15th, his 18th birthday, he decided to buy a lottery ticket. With a 1 in 4 million chance, he won 3.4 million dollars before he even started college. The money did not change his plans for after high school, as he still attended college for engineering. After he was done with college, he did what he has been telling himself he would do ever since he was a little boy. He bought a beautiful mansion off the Coast of Southern California. He achieved his goal. More and more people whom he had never talked to in high school started reaching out to him and asking to "catch up." It even seemed like his friends were trying to get closer to him and they started acting fake. While this attention was flattering to James and produced 'feel-good' hormones, it only lasted for a little while. The saddest part of achieving his goal was the moment he realized that he didn't do it for himself; he did it to impress other people. The reasoning behind your goal can make or break the satisfaction you get from accomplishing it.

If James would have created the goal of becoming a millionaire for himself (i.e. with the reasoning that he wanted to be financially independent, never have to stress about money, etc.) he would have not only felt accomplished when he reached his goal, but achieving his goal would've meant more to him, therefore he would've been even more fulfilled. Not only was James unfulfilled, but he was also upset because he started to feel more lonely. This happened when his family, friends, and acquaintances started focusing more on his money and status than on his personality and who he really was. In James' slightly far-fetched story, another reason to why he didn't feel successful was partially due to the fact that he did not work to earn his money. When he realized that he had nothing to work for, he lost his motivation and purpose.

Another common misconception is that success is easily measured by how many connections you have on LinkedIn or how many likes or followers you may get on your social media profiles. Personally, before I got the idea to write this book, I would always look at people who did well in business and would automatically assume that they have the most successful lives. What I have learned through my research and interviews is that just because people like Elon Musk and Bill Gates are extremely smart and successful in business, it would never be fair for me to assume that they consider themselves successful in life (whether they do or not).

"Business success may or may not correlate to the success of one's life. Working hard in business or as a parent can both be stepping stones into doing something greater. Turning around one life could have a residual impact for generations to come." - Bart Starr Jr.

Don't form yourself with the idea of impressing others on their scale of success, rather perform to your own standards and goals - the ones that might not sound "good" to other people. When others tell us about how they have achieved success and how we can achieve it for ourselves by following their steps, it can be tough to resist the urge to do exactly as they say. Yes, their steps that they tell you to follow are probably exactly how they achieved their success, but that's just it. They are *THEIR* ways to success, not YOURS.

Act on It!

Set a goal and create a compelling reason why
you want to reach it!

6

Success Versus Happiness

One overarching theme that I noticed while completing my interviews was that as people grow older, they realize that it isn't a matter of being "successful OR happy," because the two become more connected. A common misconception that is held when we are young is that we will become happy once we achieve a certain level of success. It isn't until we become a millionaire, billionaire, or a person of power that we acquire a final sense of satisfaction and contentment. This mindset disrupts our ability to live a truly happy and fulfilling life. I personally believe that when you are happy and you find purpose in why you do what you do, you are successful.

"For me, it is all about reputation, respect, and a healthy passion for having a life worth living." - Kevin Hermening

Many times, people find themselves getting caught up in the hedonic treadmill.

The hedonic treadmill, also known as hedonic adaptation, is a term that was originally coined by two psychologists, Brickman and Campbell. This term is used to describe the human tendency for keeping a relatively stable happiness level. Positive and negative changes will occur and either increase or decrease our mood, but after the initial emotion we experience, we will always return back to our stable emotional state. This is why material things will never sustain us - no matter how "great" it may be or how special the circumstance it may seem. Hedonic adaptation begins when we are young, and it has been something that follows each of us as we grow older.

Charlie is a ten-year-old boy and he is in the store with his mom helping her shop. They are getting groceries for dinner this week. He looks to his left and he sees the *Turbo Blaster 3000*. This isn't just *any* toy, this is the world's coolest toy water gun and he *has* to have it. If he doesn't, his life will be incomplete, and if he does, he will be happy forever. He begs his mom for the toy and explains to her why it is so important to get. After about 5 minutes of constant nagging, Charlie's mom finally says "fine, put it in the cart." He takes it home eager to use it and after about six months, he forgets about it. Yeah, it was cool at the time, but now he is older and a toy water gun is too childish. Now he needs a BB gun. His friend from school has one and it looks super fun. Charlie begs his mom for the BB gun and explains to her why this is so important to him. She asks him "Charlie, I thought you loved that *Turbo Blaster 3000* I got for you six months ago. What's wrong with that?" "But Mom, this is different. This is way cooler." She initially says no, but after a lot of persistent pleases, she gives in and buys him one for his birthday. "Wow, thanks mom! This is awesome! I love you!" he says to her. He can't seem to get enough of his new BB gun, and he practices shooting targets with it every day after school. A few years pass, and he is now a sophomore in high school. Now everyone at his school has a BB gun and, according to his friend Oliver, BB guns aren't cool anymore. Charlie shows up to school one day and sees a circle of people around Oliver. "What's happening? Is he okay?" Charlie asks to the group hoping someone would answer. After repeating his question a few times, Charlie's classmate, Justin, responded "Dude you have to check this out. Oliver got the new $1,000 smartphone with face recognition and a holographic display! It's so cool." Charlie goes into the circle to check it out. "Wow, that is really cool, I wish my mom would buy me one of those," he thought to himself. He knew that if he had that smartphone, he would at least be the second coolest kid in the sophomore class, but asking his mom to buy it was out of the question. Although, he thought to himself "Maybe if I get a job I can make enough money to buy it myself. If I get a job that pays $10 an hour and I work for about 100 hours, I will have enough money to buy it - give or take a few factors. Anyways, that's a lot of hours, but maybe if I discussed the plan with my mom she would consider helping me out." Charlie talks to his mom and she is hesitant at first, but finally says "I see that you are putting a lot of thought into this, so I would be willing to give you $200 for the phone, as long as you get the job and put the work into it." Charlie is ecstatic and ready to start applying for jobs. After a few weeks, he gets a job at a local factory and he is able to start working right away. He finally saved up enough money to buy the phone. They go to the store and pick it up, and he is so excited to use it.

Charlie is very happy with his purchase and he becomes one of the "cool kids" at his school.

Six months later and the new smartphone comes out. Oliver comes to school with it the next day. This phone is even cooler than the last and makes Charlie's phone seem like nothing.

As you can guess, the cycle continues.

Charlie wants the new phone,
Charlie gets the new phone,
The new phone gets boring.

Charlie wants a car,
Charlie gets the car,
The car gets boring.

Charlie wants a new car,
Charlie gets the new car,
The new car gets boring.

Charlie wants a big house,
Charlie gets a big house,
The big house gets boring.

The lesson that we learn when understanding the hedonic treadmill is that material things will never be enough. This can be difficult to understand when we are young because when we get things, our brain releases 'feel-good' hormones called endorphins, which give us a sense of happiness and excitement. These material things may be making us 'happy' in the short term, but we cannot get this confused with long term happiness and fulfillment.

Material things will never be enough to sustain our happiness. When people view success on a one-dimensional and superficial level, they assume that it is the key to happiness because we are finally going to get to a point where we can have anything that we have ever wanted - or at least, everything we have ever *thought* we wanted. Many people tend to think that this success is what will finally sustain us, but in my opinion, the idea of "success" that revolves around fame, status, and power is really just a higher level of the hedonic treadmill.

When we search for happiness, we look everywhere where happiness is not. I hate to be cheesy, but happiness does not come from material things or even this type of "success" that surrounds superficial ideas, it really does come from within. We search and strive to gain physical things because it seems so simple: When we have things we want, we will be happy, so we just have to buy those things in order to have a fulfilling life.

When it seems like this last idea of being "successful" will finally supply our needs and wants, we reach it only to come to the realization that it just keeps feeding the fire in the vicious cycle of hedonic adaptation.

I noticed that when I asked my friends the loaded question "would you rather be successful or happy?" the common answer was either "I would probably say successful because when I become successful, I will be happy" or "Definitely happy, because not all rich people live great lives" (this answer implies that they perceive success through money - which comes from what society teaches us). If I would've asked the question "Do you consider success and happiness to be two separate things?" I may have gotten different answers. I noticed that the older the person was who I interviewed, the more their answer revolved around relationships, family, and living an overall happy life.

As a teenager, I am fortunate to be able spend time with my family and friends. In my conversations with my friends and peers about their futures, their focus tended to revolve around the things they would have, as opposed to their relationships.

During my conversations with the people I interviewed and other adults, I noticed that when speaking about success, their ideas typically revolved more around the importance of relationships and the time they wish they had with their family and friends.

"I believe that it is quite common to consider success as the attainment of a lot of fame or fortune. Certainly, having money prospectively brings about a more comfortable lifestyle. But that version of success should never be mistaken by the idea that a truly successful person is one who has deep relationships with family and friends." - Kevin Hermening

We have all heard the cliché quote "life's a journey, not a destination," by Ralph Waldo Emerson. The problem with clichés is that since they are common well-known phrases, they tend to be overlooked. You would think that since they are said so often they would be more understood - but it is exactly the opposite. The more we become familiar with something, the less we continue to think about it on a deeper level and question what it could really mean for us. So again, when I say that "life is a journey, not a destination," I really challenge you to think about what that means. I like to relate this to the common idea of success that revolves around the ideas of status, wealth, fame, and power. I do this because a lot of people go through life telling themselves that once they get "this" or once they achieve "that," they will become successful. When in reality, some of the most successful people have realized that it is not necessarily about what they have specifically accomplished or earned, but instead it is about learning and understanding that success comes when you are able to start using the words "success" and "happiness" interchangeably.

Think About It

Would you rather be successful or happy? Why?

Do you consider success and happiness to be two separate things? Why?

Think about something you bought that you thought would make you happy and didn't.

Act on It!

Make a list of the top ten things that make you happy!

7

Everyone is Fallible

Newsflash! Adults who are considered to be successful do not always have everything figured out like you may think they do - or at least how I thought they did. In reality, these "successful" adults are just trying their best with what they are given. Yes, it is true that when we turn 18 we officially become an "adult," however, there is no time that comes when we have to become an expert on everything.

When I first decided to write this book, I was terrified to talk to older "successful" people, especially in business because I have always put them on a pedestal. When I first began to reach out to people, I hoped that they would prefer to do an email interview, because I knew that emails would be much easier. I could proofread what I would say, I wouldn't stumble over my words, and I could hide my nerves. Although, I also knew that when I communicate over the phone or in person I would be able to get a better understanding of what the person is saying by their body language and tone.

My first in-person interview was with Bart Starr Jr., and I probably made it apparent to him that he was the first person I interviewed. Before the interview, I was really scared; I would get very nervous when it came to talking to business professionals and adults in general. I was scared that they would judge me and know that I was nervous. Now looking back on it, I have no idea why I was always so timid in those situations. I understand why I cared a lot about what adults think, but before having those experiences, I would have never realized how putting them on a pedestal is actually destructive to the conversation. Once I was able to realize that (most) adults aren't scary after all and that they are simply other humans who make mistakes, I was able to communicate my ideas effectively and listen with purpose.

"I've made lots of mistakes, but learned from them all...I will keep making them, and I will keep learning." - Susan Lang, Vice President, General Manager and Co-Owner of "From the Forest"

One thing I noticed during each of the interviews was that every little mistake they made (whether simply messing up their words, spilling food on themselves when eating, knocking over their chair when they stood up, etc.), each of their mistakes were magnified because I had the perception that adults don't make mistakes.

One of the things that stops certain generations from effectively communicating and listening to each other is the preconceived notions that we hold in our heads. Once we realize that everyone makes mistakes and everyone is fallible, we are able to connect and understand people better. I think Hannah Montana said it best: *"Everybody makes mistakes, everybody has those days, everybody knows what, what I'm talkin' 'bout, everybody gets that way."*

Pencil vs. Pen Theory

As a kid, we are taught to write in pencil because if we make a mistake on the paper, we can simply erase it and start over. We get used to this, which makes us feel comfortable with making mistakes since they are easy to erase. As we grow up, we get more freedom to use pens, but many of us do not make the switch until we have to. When you use a pen and make a mistake, you can cover it with white-out, let it dry, and write over it, but it still will not look professional. This is typically because we know that it is easier to correct a mistake in pencil than it is to in pen, and this alone can put a subconscious pressure in our heads that we can only use pens when we are 100% confident that we won't make a mistake. Once we become adults, we learn that we have to use pens in most of the things we do because when it comes to important paperwork, it is both unprofessional and the writing could be altered, which may have irreversible consequences.

(Note: I am not saying that writing utensils are the reason why kids think adults are infallible, rather it is to give a relatable example)

The comparison of pencils/kids to pens/adults when trying to understand if anyone really has anything figured out can be misleading. This analogy shows us that there is a point in our life where we are forced to grow up (when we are forced to use pens). Although, just because we grow up does not mean that we ever stop making mistakes.

As a child, we are taught:
"Listen to adults"
"Always respect your elders"
"Never disrespect your teacher"
and the list goes on...

These phrases teach us that we must listen to adults and do as we are told (valid). The only problem with this is that sometimes it can establish a false sense reality that adults are infallible. We should listen to our elders - not with a presumption that they know everything, but instead with the understanding that they have had more experiences than us and they have so much that we could learn from. It is important to understand that we should always respect our elders, but also keep in mind that our elders are humans too.

"Old people are just young people who grew up."
- *Kyle Willkom,* keynote speaker and author of *The Thinking Dilemma* and *Wake Up Call*

You probably took a quick glance at this quote and thought something along the lines of "well yeah, obviously," but I encourage you to take time to really think about it.

We sometimes assume that successful adults are just naturally good at life, but in reality they still trip, spill oatmeal on themselves, accidentally knock over their chairs at dinner, and mix up their words when speaking.

Who is someone you look up to?

Act on It!

Write down three characteristics that you find admirable that you would like to be known for.

Part 3

Pillars of Achievement

The phrase "The Pillars of ____" is common in the literary world. *The Five Pillars of a Meaningful Life, The Five Pillars of Faith, The Five Pillars of a Happy Family, The Five Pillars of Success, The Five Pillars of Character,* and so on. It is interesting to see that each of the "Pillars" are all very different. How they are represented changes from source to source. This is surely stated because they are all a matter of perspective - and no two people's perspectives are exactly the same.

I would like to make it apparent that I am not calling this my *Five Pillars of Success.* Instead for myself, this is about achievement. Although achievement and success are closely related and overlap, in my opinion, they are not the same. Achievement is a one-dimensional figure attached to a goal or end result, while success is more of an all-encompassing feeling, state of mind, and how one views their own way of life. I believe that success comes when you are who you want to be and you find purpose in why you do what you do. Achievement is what happens when you accomplish your goals, and success comes into play when you fully understand why you made the goals you made in order to benefit your life as a whole.

This is why, after sharing what my *Five Pillars of Achievement* are, I encourage you to find your own *Pillars of Achievement*. You may feel the need to add something that is important or relevant to your own goals; possibly something such as natural talent, passion, or attitude. Perhaps you even take something out or replace it. You may even have the same pillars, but with different reasoning. Again, it's all a matter of perspective and it comes back to your primary vision of achievement.

8

Pillar 1: "Hard Work Prevails"

You hear it everywhere: you can't be successful without hard work and dedication. We all know that one kid who was once a child prodigy. For example, an 8th grade basketball player, let's call him Jack, who always got the ball passed to him because everyone knew that he could make every shot with ease. Sometimes people called Jack a ball hog, but in the end, all that mattered was whether the team won or lost - and he was the determining factor. Senior year in high school rolls around and he is on the bench for almost every game. Why? Because everyone caught up to him. Jack was the first one in his age group to "develop," and once he realized that he was so much better than everyone else, he thought to himself "what's the point of even working hard if I am already so much better than everyone else?" This mindset is what caused him to start slacking - not to mention the work ethic and later development of his teammates. It was Jack's last year of high school and his team made it to the state finals. Ben, Jack's teammate, rolled his ankle in the 2nd half. It was Jack's turn to go in; the score was close. There were two minutes left. Now one. The score was 60-61 and the opposing team was up. An opposing player fouls on Jack, and he now has two chances on the free-throw line with 5 seconds left. Making one ties the game and making both almost guarantees them to win. He shoots. The ball bounces off the rim and back. Now Jack starts to feel the pressure. He takes a breath and shoots the second one. Everyone in the audience holds their breath for what seems to be forever. It rolls around the inside of the rim and swings out. His head goes down in embarrassment and disappointment. With only 4 seconds left and the other team holding the ball, Jack's team didn't have a chance. The team went home without a plaque, and nobody talked to Jack on the way home. He started thinking to himself "How would it have been different if I would've worked harder and pushed myself, rather than solely relying on natural talent?" Not only would Jack have made himself proud, but he also could have helped lead his team to victory during his most important year of high school. We all know that it was not only Jack's fault that they lost the game, but he knew that if he would have just worked a little harder, he could have made a difference.

9

Pillar 2: "A Little Luck Can't Hurt"

No extremely "famous" singer or actor would be where they are today without a little bit of luck. Don't get me wrong; they are all very talented. Although, without recognizing opportunities, it would be difficult for them to reach the same level.

When people say "you just got lucky," it sounds almost as though they are trying to downplay your accomplishment. However, being lucky is not necessarily a bad thing at all. It means that, with your preparation, you had a really great opportunity in front of you that you took advantage of.

Imagine two aspiring singers: Jessica and Lindsey. Both have been singing ever since they were very young and they are very talented. Since they were twelve years old, every Tuesday they perform at a small music cafe in their hometown. They take turns each week, and on the 14th of October, it was Lindsey's turn. It also just so happened that a recording producer was in town that day gathering ideas for his most recent project and wanted to grab a coffee. When he walked into the cafe, he saw her sing and was blown away. Lindsey then got an offer to work with him and she decided to accept. It was a risk that she knew she had to take if she wanted a shot at stardom. She seized the great opportunity ahead of her and worked hard with the producer to get better. In two years, she already had three hits and was able to make more connections than ever through her work. She gained a following and a rapidly growing fan base. While she was consistently working hard as a singer before the opportunity came to her, having the courage to take the risk with his offer was what specifically helped her get where she wanted to be. Jessica was just as good, if not even better than Lindsey. The difference between them came in just one opportunity.

10

Pillar 3: "It's Not What You Know, It's Who You Know"

Networking and people skills go somewhat hand in hand with opportunity. You probably know the common phrase "It's not what you know, it's who you know," which almost directly implies that you could be the most intelligent and creative person in the world, but if you do not have the right connections, you will never be able to get your dream job or find success. While this statement seems like a fairly aggressive approach, it does have some truth to it. When you know certain people, you have a greater chance to get "lucky" with opportunities more often. This does NOT mean that you absolutely *have* to bear incredible networking skills to earn opportunities, although it definitely does help.

Another myth is that you have to be born into a position where it is easy to get in contact with other people. For this example, we will take Bart Starr Jr. He knows a lot of people through his dad, but without his own willingness to branch out and make his personal connections, he would not have been able to earn the positive network and respect that he has gained throughout his life. You can only rely on another person's help for so long. You do not have to currently be someone "known" or "important" to make connections.

When my mom first met Bart Starr Jr., she was attending an event at Lambeau Field where he was giving a speech. On her way out, she saw Bart Starr Jr. walking in the parking lot. She took the opportunity to walk up to him, introduce herself, and invite him to speak at an event in Wausau, Wisconsin. He agreed, and a connection was made. If she wouldn't have had the initial willingness to reach out, she would have never gained the connection, and I potentially wouldn't have had the ability to get his contact information to interview him.

It is important to take risks by putting yourself in situations to find opportunity. It is also important to keep in mind that even if you do not necessarily know the "right" people, you can still get "lucky" when opportunities present themselves.

11

Pillar 4: "Know Thyself"

If you are unable to be honest with yourself by knowing your strengths, weaknesses, passions, dislikes, etc., you will not be able to properly grow and become the best version of whoever you wish to be.

Jayde is a Senior in high school. She has no idea what she wants to do for a career or which path she should take when it comes to her future. She is a great student and always exceeds expectations when it comes to class work, extracurriculars, and community service. While her close friends and family would agree that Jayde has a very extroverted, loud, and funny personality, Jayde is not completely confident in herself and does not know what she wants to do with her life.

She has done some research on well-paying jobs with positive outlooks, but she has not put much effort into her own true personal reflection; she has not taken the time to think about or write down what she deeply believes she is good at, enjoys doing, considers successful, etc. As she grows up, she attends Columbia University to study law. She does what she needs to do to get by and it comes fairly easy to her. When Jayde turns 25, she gets married to a man whom she loves dearly, they buy a house in North Carolina, and she finds a job as a corporate lawyer. When Jayde turns 28, she begins to believe that there is no purpose in the work she is doing. She feels that she is not making meaningful connections with people and she is just putting in hours solely for the sake of having a decent paycheck. Jayde is not living up to her full potential. This is not because she doesn't put in enough effort and work into her job as a corporate lawyer, but it is because she is not working in a place that maximizes her strengths and allows her to be passionate towards what she puts her time into daily.

Now it's too late for Jayde to switch jobs...or is it? Yes, being already settled down after having a family and stable job is not necessarily the "ideal" time to change your entire career path, but are our lives ever "ideal?"

Luckily for Jayde, she is able to have an honest conversation with her husband about this predicament. He said that he will support her as she looks for other career paths, but with one catch: she has to make sure that this next career is one that she is 100% confident in and it must be her final decision. While this seems like a simple agreement, thoughts and questions start running through Jayde's mind. "How do I choose a new career when I don't even know what I want? How do I know if the career I choose is the right one for me? What if something happens where I end up not liking it?"

After asking herself these questions, she does what most 21st century millennials with a computer would do: she asks Google. Jayde finds what seems to be billions of links to different personal assessments, books, podcasts, videos, and articles on how to know yourself and what career is the best fit. She does her research and realizes that she has to be 100% brutally honest when learning about herself. It seems simple and obvious, but when she really thought about it, she realized that her problem was that she was only seeing herself how she wanted others to see her. It wasn't until she fully grasped the concept of being honest with yourself that she was able to make progress on where she was going.

She takes a few different personality tests, and they all seem to give her slightly different, but overlapping results. From this, she learns that she is a great communicator and she has an extroverted, imaginative, and generous personality. She begins searching for professions that would well suit her. She comes across a few such as "Human Resources Professional, Psychologist, Counselor, and Coach." None of which clearly stood out. As she keeps looking, she sees "Teacher," which reminds her of how much she enjoys babysitting and being with children. As she looks more into it, she realizes that this might be the right fit for her. She tells her husband and they understand that if she decides to become a teacher, there will be certain ramifications regarding her decision. For example, they may think about getting a smaller house to accommodate for their new income. She also would get the summers off which would be helpful, especially if they have kids later on in life. Once she finally understands all that would come from this change, she makes her final decision to become a teacher.

Jayde discusses her decision with her loved ones and they all support her. She is ecstatic to begin her new journey, and she looks for other part-time employment that would be available to her during schooling. Jayde graduates with her teaching degree and gets a full-time job at a nearby elementary school. She loves going to work every day and never feels like she is being forced into things that she doesn't enjoy. Jayde now feels almost as though she was set free from a life she never would have wanted to live.

If this story sounds familiar to you because you are in a place where you are putting your time and effort into things that you don't enjoy...fix it! It is never too late to change your life in a positive way. It is easy to fall into the trap of saying that you are fine with the life you currently live, but don't lie to yourself! If you're great, say you're great. If you're unhappy, say you're unhappy - but DO NOT SAY YOU ARE FINE IF YOU ARE UNHAPPY. By doing this, you get tricked into allowing yourself to not do anything about it. This is one of the most destructive things we can do to ourselves and the world around us because it does not allow us to maximize our full potential. It may not always be the easiest to take action, but it is worth the work to live a happy and fulfilling life. There is nobody telling you how you have to live your life, so live it the way that you want to!

12

Pillar 5: "Without Goals, Where Are You Going?"

If you are unsure of where you want to go, do you expect to end up in a place that you want to be? Setting SMART (Specific, Measurable, Achievable, Relevant, Timely) goals creates focus and accountability. That focus and accountability exceeds tremendously once you take the time to write your goals down. According to Dr. Gail Matthews, a psychology professor at the Dominican University in California, the likelihood of achieving your goals increases by 42% once you write them down.

In our brains, we all have a left and right hemisphere. Our right hemisphere is known as the more creative, holistic, and intuitive part of the brain while the left hemisphere is more logical, analytical, and factual. When we develop goals and think about them, we use the right side of our brain. We are very visual creatures, and once we take the time to physically write down our goals, it allows us to see the goal for what it truly is. In simple terms, thinking about our goals uses only the right side of our brain, but once we write them down, it forces our whole brain to get actively involved. By putting our goals on paper, the left and right hemispheres of the brain come together and give us a much higher chance of achieving them. By writing down our goals, we are able to clarify what we want, get motivated, and see our progress.

If you aren't already regularly writing down your goals, it becomes easy for them to stray from your mind. When you think of something that you have to pick up from the grocery store for dinner, chances are, you write it down. Why? Because if you don't write it down, you will forget about it. When you are at school and get a homework assignment, chances are, you write it down. Why? Because if you don't write it down, you will forget about it. When you are at work and remember that you have to send an important email out when you get home, chances are, you write it down. Why? Because if you don't write it down, you will forget about it. So, let's ask ourselves: Why aren't we writing down our goals? Our personal goals are just as, if not even more important to us than if we get all of the ingredients for our dinner one night or forget to do a small homework assignment. So again, why aren't we writing down the things that are most important to us?

Samantha is a teenage girl who really wants to write a book before she goes off to college. She is very driven, but is very involved within her school and extracurricular activities. As the days turn into weeks, the weeks turn into months, and she keeps saying to herself "I'll work on it tomorrow" or "I'm not sure where to start." Before she even realizes it, Samantha graduates. What was once a vision turned into a lost cause. If Samantha would have made her book a priority, she could have put together a list of goals and tasks to accomplish it. Without dividing a big vision into small and manageable tasks, it will seem far-fetched and impossible to reach. What you may not initially realize is that Samantha represents myself.

When I got the idea to write this book, I was swamped with volleyball leagues, softball, DECA, FCCLA, Student Senate, NHS, my jobs, etc. One thing that was a vital key to finishing this book was understanding what my priorities were, making goals, and scheduling tasks accordingly. Time management and getting rid of time wasters, such as spending countless hours looking through irrelevant social media, also played a large role in accomplishing my goal.

While we are living our lives, we get busy, and that is why we write down the little things that we have to get done in order to not forget about them. There is a major difference between the little things we have to get done and our goals. They are both important to us, but the major difference is that our "must do" tasks have strict timelines and our personal goals usually do not. The majority of people will procrastinate on things they have to do by waiting until the last second to do them, but they will still eventually get it done. This is because when things have deadlines, they also have built-in consequences. For example, if you want to eat spaghetti for dinner and you forget to buy the noodles from the store, the built-in consequence is that you will not get to eat what you want for dinner. If you are a student and forgot to do your homework, the built-in consequence may be that you don't do well on the test, which could affect your grade in the class.

Since our personal goals are ones that we set for ourselves, there are usually no deadlines - therefore, there are no built-in consequences. Although, just because there are no built-in consequences, does not mean that there are no consequences. The consequences for never accomplishing your personal goals can be less noticeable, yet even more destructive to your overall well-being. When we aren't accomplishing our goals, we are not maximizing our full potential.

Many people say that it is important to tell others about your personal goals or publicly state them via channels such as social media. This follows the logic that you become more likely to achieve something when others are aware and able to keep you accountable. When we develop a goal and write it down, we get very excited to tell our friends about it with the thought that they will be proud of us and be able to keep us on track. In reality, unless you have a friend that is extremely invested in you and your time, they are probably already too focused on accomplishing their own goals to be thinking about keeping you on track of yours. The other issue with publicly stating your goals is that it can create a false sense of accomplishment. When you tell someone about your goal, the usual response is comprised of encouraging words and praise. The response that comes from this generally makes you feel good, almost as though you have already attained what it was that you were telling them about. Depending on the goal, it may or may not be beneficial to tell friends or family members.

Imagine Chase, a 27-year-old, attended an exceptionally enlightening seminar on the importance of healthy eating and exercise. He came back feeling changed and ready to start his new health journey. He knew that in order for him to actually accomplish his dream, he had to develop SMART goals. He also learned the importance of physically writing reminders on paper to keep him motivated to never stray from his journey. His goal was to lose 50 pounds, and he wasn't going to follow the classic "Beach Body in 10 Days!" or "Lose Weight with This Easy Pill - No Dieting or Exercising!" While these seemed tempting to try, he knew that they were too good to be true and he would quickly regain the weight back. Instead, he would achieve his goal by following an eating plan and going to the gym every morning for a year. It was two weeks into the process and Chase was on perfect pace to reach his goal. He was so excited that he decided to let all of his friends know about his progress. His friends were very impressed with him as they praised him with kind and encouraging words. Chase came to feel genuinely accomplished and proud of himself. Because of this positive interaction with his friends, Chase decided that he deserved a day off to reward himself for all of his hard work. He then felt that since he had taken one day off, it wouldn't hurt him to take the whole weekend off. After that weekend, Chase got a big project at work that had to be done on the following Friday. He figured that it would be in his best interest to take the week off and work on this project. "One week wouldn't hurt, right?" Chase said to himself. Long story short, one week turned into two weeks, two weeks turned into one month, and before he knew it, his eating plan and exercising came to a halt. Not only did this have an effect on his physical health, but it also prevented Chase from setting certain goals in the future. He figured that if he couldn't complete the simple "eat healthy and exercise" for a year, he wouldn't be able to set what he saw as bigger and more complex goals.

Perhaps Chase's story sounds familiar to you. Everyone has their different ways that work when trying to accomplish a goal, so I deeply encourage you to find your own. Personally, I find working month by month and keeping my goals to myself works best. When finding what works for you, maybe you need to tell people, develop specific to-do lists each day, or create more incentives for yourself. Whatever it is, make sure that you find what works best for *you*.

<u>*Think About It*</u>

What are your Pillars of Achievement?

Act on It!

Share your Pillars of Achievement with a person you trust.

Part 4

Conclusion

While concluding my research, I was able to learn a lot about how everything works together in order to create a successful life. Although, your idea of what a successful life looks like is still a mystery to me. While I was able to get a better grasp on the big ideas that people understand about success as they get older, I was amazed to see how everything connected as I created my own definition of success.

One connection that I made was between opportunities and authenticity. Opportunities come and go, and you won't get the same opportunities as the person next to you. For example, perhaps someone tells you exactly how they became successful and they even give you their steps to follow in order to do the same. The steps were accurate in that they *are* how they achieved their "success," but no matter what the steps are, the world is constantly changing and all of the factors that go into each person's success is different. This is why you cannot compare yourself to others; their opportunities will always be different than yours. Opportunities don't come the same for everyone, so even if you listen to how someone else came to be successful, your journey will be different; it's a different time, you have had different experiences, and chances are, you have different definitions of success.

"Success has always and will always look, feel, and seem different to everyone. In my opinion, money, fame, and accolades do not mean someone is successful, yet many others do see that as the appearance of success. I do think at some point in life I also saw these traits as being the epitome of success and I won't tell you that receiving awards or acknowledgement for doing my job well is unwelcomed. Yet, it is my personal life that I look to and check for my measurement of success. Is my family happy? Are we financially stable? Am I a good friend? Do my students respect me and learn from me? Do people consider me a good person? If I can answer yes to these questions, then I feel successful." - *Deidre Bradford, High School English Teacher*

Another characteristic I noticed while conducting my interviews was humility. This made me start thinking about the idea of humility vs. arrogance. Arrogant people tend to act as though they are above others. Therefore, they do not listen; therefore, they do not learn. They do not see certain opportunities that they would if they understood that you can learn so much from the people around you. Humility was a trait that I was able to notice, but it was not something that was greatly talked about - as it shouldn't be.

The ideas that inspired this book did not only come from the specific people who I interviewed, but they also came from plenty of experiences and conversations that I have had with other people as well. While I didn't have formal "interviews" with kids, teenagers, and other adults, I did have many other conversations in which I asked similar questions regarding people's views of success. I recorded the general responses and my thoughts about each answer. These experiences allowed me to get a greater understanding of other people's perceptions of success.

One example was when I was talking with my friend's dad. I asked him "If you have a lot of money, does that mean you are successful?"
He replied, "No, not necessarily." Then I asked him, "Okay, so what is success?" He replied, "I would say that success is different for everyone."

I then asked, "So how would *you* define success? What is success to *you*?"

He replied, "Well, I think having a happy and healthy family, having a job that I love, etc."

A little later, I asked him another question that was inspired by Jay Forte, "Would you rather be successful or happy?"

He then replied with "I would rather be happy because even some of the richest people on this earth are very depressed." While his statement is very true, him saying this reaffirmed the subconscious connections he made when thinking about success.

I think that everyone knows or has heard that "money isn't everything" and "material things don't determine your success," but what I have noticed is that it's not until you grow older that you actually start to believe and genuinely are able to grasp these thoughts. Some adults haven't even figured this out yet. When we are young, we may know these things, but as we get older we begin to actually believe them.

"I personally hate having "things," but what you spend your money on is not a matter of morals or ethics, it is simply a matter of taste." - Jim Frings, CEO of G3 Industries

If you haven't already noticed, I personally believe that just having a lot of money, a big house, and expensive cars does not mean that you are successful. Keep in mind: that is *my* opinion. It would sound pretty bad if I started this book out by stating that you have to create your own definition of success without letting anyone else's opinion directly influence you, only to later say that your definition of success cannot be related to money, a big house, or expensive cars.

If your idea of success revolves around wealth, great.

If your idea of success revolves around maintaining good relationships in your life, great.

If your idea of success revolves around being a productive person, great.

If your idea of success revolves around having a healthy family, great.

If your idea of success revolves around having a big house, great.

But if you live your life working towards one of these things in hopes to become successful and you either:

a. Don't know why

   or

b. Aren't doing it for yourself

NOT GREAT!!!

The goal of this book is not to tell you how you should see success, but it is to share with you what I have learned about how people's ideas of success have developed as they have grown older. In the process, I hope it allows you to make your own definition of success more mature and thought out. I am *not* saying what your definition should be. I *am* saying that whatever your definition is - make sure that you know why, and make sure it is important to *you*.

Another specific example of a time when I got the perspective of a teenager was when I asked my friend to write down his answer to the question: "Which would you rather have: success or happiness?" His reply was this: "Well, let's see, having success will usually give you happiness, but happiness may be more important because at least you're happy even if you may not succeed. So... it's about a horse apiece." By saying it is "a horse apiece," he was saying that, in a way, they are more or less equal. So, if you could understand the rest of that, I believe that his idea behind the point was that success will usually give you happiness, but you can be happy even if you aren't successful.

I noticed the general trend that arose when asking younger people about how they saw success was that success is something that is not typically thought deeply about, so being asked questions about it is strange. Although, once they have time to really think about the topic, the main ideas were: success is different for everyone, it comes when you achieve your goals, and success is getting what you need and want in life. I notice that most people will not come out and say that success means that you have a big house and a lot of money, but having a big house and money tends to be subconsciously linked to success, based off of society's unrealistic ideals.

Everybody wants to be admired by everyone, but not everyone can be admired by everyone - because everyone admires different types of people.

Looking back on the experiences that I have had with the interviews and conversations, I am extremely grateful for how much I have learned through this experience. For those of you who know me and know how

I ask questions, you probably know that I tend to ask a lot of self-reflection and understanding-types of questions. When I ask these questions, I do not usually think about how I personally would answer them. When I formatted the questions for the interviews, I read through them and I was curious to see what my answers would be, so I thought for a while...I couldn't answer them. By the time that I was getting close to finishing up this book, I decided to look back on the questions. I went through them and I was able to thoroughly answer them with purpose. You may be thinking to yourself sarcastically "Wow, what an accomplishment. You could answer some questions." Personally, I think that this alone is a great representation of how much I have learned through this whole experience. Once you are able to answer each of those questions truthfully and thoughtfully, I believe that in itself is an accomplishment.

What I found to be really interesting is that the three main ideas that I got from the people who I interviewed were not the common ideas that came across when I read articles about "what every successful person lives by." I felt that these especially interesting because they are specific unique ideas that play a crucial role in finding your definition of success - not the obvious "just work hard and you'll be successful." (Don't get me wrong because, as you could see in my *Pillars of Achievement section*, I value hard work tremendously.)

Everyone I spoke with brought so much value to this process, and I would like to say a quick thank you to everyone who had a part in this book - whether you realized it or not. Your thoughts, ideas, and words all have played a tremendous role in my journey. Again, thank you.

Now, I encourage you to ask yourself the questions I asked the people who I interviewed:

1) How would you define success today compared to when you were younger?

2) What are the key attributes that helped you get to where you are today?

3) Who helped you the most along the way? Did you have any specific mentors or teachers who made an impact? What did you learn from them?

4) What is the best piece of advice you have ever gotten?

5) What is your favorite book?

6) If you could go back in time, what would you want to tell your younger self?

7) If you could change one thing in the world, what would it be?

8) Do you consider yourself to be an introvert or an extrovert?

9) What was the one thing that impacted you the most?

10) What was the biggest mistake you have ever made and/or if you could do anything differently, what would it be?

A Letter to High School Students

Dear High School Student,

In high school, you are rewarded for conforming to a set standard. The more that you are like the "ideal" student, the more you are praised, rewarded, and given opportunities. We are taught that the "ideal" student is the student who gets good grades and doesn't get into trouble. Well, how do you get good grades and stay out of trouble? You need to be able to recite back what the teacher tells you in the form of homework and tests. Seems pretty simple, doesn't it? The only problem with this is that it is so easy to recite what other people think - and what does that teach you? When we don't question why we are doing what we are doing, we don't have control over what we are doing. Don't get me wrong, it is important to listen to what others tell you to do, especially if that person is in charge of you - whether that be at school or work. Although, if everyone in the world spent their whole life solely doing what other people told them to do, what type of world would we be living in?

Now, this is not a letter to explain what is wrong with our educational system today. Rather, it is to help give a perspective about why success in school will not always predict success in life. The way that most schools are set up allows people who conform to succeed, and people who are unique to either do poorly or dismiss their own perspective and conform. While many teachers are great at encouraging creativity, it can be difficult if the system does not reward individualism.

The world beyond school demands many different types of people, as it tends to reward those who are unique and diverse in their thought. This is because people who question the world will be the people who change the world. The scale used to measure success in school is in some ways the flipped scale of what is used in real life.

Schools tend to make kids feel as though they have to be completely knowledgeable in all areas. To get a 4.0, you need to do extremely well in all of your classes, regardless of the subject. While the different learning techniques that are used in each subject allow the students' general learning processes to grow, that does not necessarily mean that students must be experts in every subject in order to triumph in their futures. As a matter of fact, while schools hold you to a certain scale of well-roundedness that will then determine your success in school, the world beyond school has no specific standard that you have to meet. Instead, it is up to you to decide what you are good at and what career fits you best. It is still very important to develop a good understanding of many subjects, but not always to the extent that the schools praise. In school, you have to follow the ideal mold, while in the "real world," you learn that you have to make your difference with your own reasons.

Everyone has either said or heard something along the lines of "But teacher, when are we EVER going to have to use this math in the real world? I already know what I want to do when I grow up, and this has nothing to do with it." The common response from the teacher is "Math is in everything, and it will follow you wherever you go - no matter what career you have." Generally, once we reach a certain age in school, we begin to question why we take so much time to learn things such as the Quadratic Formula and how to find the area of a Rhombus when we:

    a. Don't plan on doing anything with math for a career

OR

    b. Can just look it up on Google

What schools don't usually tell us is that we are partially right. Perhaps you won't end up using these specific math formulas when you grow up, or maybe you will. The one thing that is inevitable is that you learn from every class you take, whether you retain the specific information the teacher is teaching or not. You learn a great deal from the actual thinking and actions that are being done in the classroom. Not only do we develop our thinking processes and gain information, but we also learn a lot about hard work and persistence when doing work that we don't particularly enjoy. In our life, we will encounter times when we don't feel like doing anything, but we don't always have a choice. School is a place that both helps us get used to that and develops all aspects of our thinking processes.

Remember: be authentic, never stop asking questions, be a lifelong learner, and create your own definition of success.

Sincerely,
Christina Wenman

"I advocate school, but I advocate education more. It seems that the most successful people have to educate themselves." - Daniel Ally

Profiles of Interviewees

*as submitted by interviewees

Tyrone M. Robinson III

Tyrone M. Robinson III is a business owner out of the Greater Philadelphia Area. His business, Opportunities 2 Serve helps businesses and entrepreneurs grow their businesses through growth and marketing strategies. Robinson is passionate about building and creating world-class organizations that significantly impact the success and satisfaction of their employees, internal and external customers, shareholders and communities. Tyrone is also a Speaker, Board Member, and Author of the book: *The Light Within Us All: Life Lessons Through Self-Discovery.*

Daniel Ally

Daniel Ally is a highly successful serial entrepreneur, consultant, and investor who has reached fortune and fame before the age of 30. He is the author of six books and courses. Daniel has given thousands of speeches in hundreds of cities. His famous TED talk has six million views. You can learn more about him on *www.danielally.com.*

Rich Poirier

Rich Poirier joined Church Mutual in April 2011 as Vice President — Claims and was promoted to Chief Operating Officer in October 2011. He was named President in 2014. He assumed his present position in January 2016. Poirier earned his Bachelor of Arts degree from Marquette University in 1983. Following graduation, he was given a direct commission in the United States Navy through its Law Education Program. Poirier earned his Juris Doctorate from Marquette University in 1986. Following law school graduation, he entered four years of active duty as a Navy judge advocate in Norfolk, Virginia. Following his discharge from active duty, Poirier continued his service in the Navy Reserves. He held a number of prestigious assignments, including two commanding officer tours. He retired in 2010 at the rank of Captain. His numerous awards and decorations include two Navy Achievement Medals, two Navy Commendation Medals, and a Meritorious Service Medal. Poirier is active in numerous civic organizations. He currently sits on the Board of Directors of Aspirus, Inc.; the NTC Foundation; the Marathon County Chapter of the Boys and Girls Club of America and the Wausau Wolf Pack Youth Lacrosse Association.

Jay Forte

Jay is the founder of The Forte Factor, a business committed to helping everyone discover, develop and live what is best in them to achieve exceptional personal and professional results. Jay is also a business and motivational speaker, certified professional coach, educator and nationally ranked Thought Leader. He is the author of *Fire Up! Your Employees and Smoke Your Competition,* and *The Greatness Zone – Know Yourself, Find Your Fit, Transform the World.* He has been the host of *The Greatness Zone* and *Get Your Kids Ready for Life* podcasts, writes for many national sites and periodicals and constantly speaks about personal and professional potential, mindfulness, performance, talent, service, and leadership. When not teaching, coaching CEOs, or helping people discover and live their Forte Factor, he writes, gardens, cooks (as any good Italian) and spends time with his partner, three adult daughters, and two grandsons. He lives in Ft Lauderdale, FL.

Deidre Bradford

Deidre K. Bradford is a well-seasoned high school English teacher in Mosinee, Wisconsin. She began her teaching career at the high-achieving campuses of Arrowhead Union High School in Hartland, Wisconsin before transitioning to Monona Grove High School located within the bubble of Madison, where she expanded her classroom skills into other areas of expertise within the world of language arts. Throughout her teaching career she has taught English 9, 10, 11 along with Honors English 10, Modern Literature, Speech, Genres of Literature, Advanced Composition, Introduction to Film and Technical Writing and Skills. Deidre has also coached girls' basketball as well as boys' and girls' volleyball throughout most of her career but stopped once she became mom.

Before starting her career as a teacher, Deidre received her Bachelor of Science from Winona State University in Winona, MN where she even tackled the game of rugby. During her second year of teaching, she decided to earn her Master of Education - Professional Development degree from the University of Wisconsin-La Crosse.

Personally, Deidre is married to her husband Dan and they have two beautiful kids, Angela and Jordy. All her life Deidre wanted to be an adoptive mom, but little did she know that was exactly how she was to become one! She enjoys all the glories and trials of raising two young kids while also working full-time...well, most of the time it's enjoyable! Deidre is originally from central Wisconsin and after spending some time in both the Madison and Milwaukee areas, she and her husband decided to raise their kids close to family. Family, her students are included in this, are and always be what drives her to be the best person, mom, wife and teacher she can be.

Bart Starr Jr.

Graduated from the University of Alabama (1980) and University of Alabama School of Law (1983). Co-founder and partner, Starr Sanders Properties (1990), a real estate firm focused on developing and managing medical office buildings. SSP was acquired by Healthcare Realty Trust, a REIT, in 1996. Founder of Performance Futures (1985), a firm designed to be a bridge between speculative investors and professional managers in the commodity futures markets. Firm eventually became Starr Enterprises and advises approximately 500 individual investors. Financial consulting and wealth management for a small number of athletes and businessmen. Supporter of numerous charities benefitting youth and education. Father to three daughters and a very proud "Papa" to grandsons, Bryan Jackson and Teddy Lambert.

Jim Frings

Jim Frings owns and operates G3 Industries, Inc., a $25 million manufacturer of custom – engineered components and assemblies. He also owns real estate investment companies engaged in multi-family housing, commercial, and industrial properties in 4 states. Jim invests in private companies in the software, entertainment, and computer hardware support industries. He also sits on several corporate and not-for-profit boards. After graduating from the School of Foreign Science at Georgetown and earning an MBA from Columbia Business

School, Jim worked for Intel where he developed and implemented technology transfers, joint ventures, and new distribution channels on six continents. In 1989, the entrepreneurial bug bit him. He turned around a small manufacturer in Oregon for a boutique PE firm and, then, in 1993 he bought the company in Wisconsin that would become G3 Industries. Young people like Christina Wenman inspire Jim. He enjoys investing in the dreams and hard work of what will become another great American generation.

Susan Lang

Susan Lang attended college at the University of Wisconsin - Madison with a degree in business. She moved to Wausau after graduation planning on getting a summer internship job at a manufacturing company before going to grad school. It was a start-up company with a lot of potential, and it convinced her to get "on the job experience" and forgo Graduate School. She has had the privilege of working hard, learning a lot, traveling the world, and collaborating with amazing people. Since the start-up, she has been involved in running, acquiring, consulting, and selling a variety of manufacturing companies in the wood processing and specialty coatings industry. She is the recipient of the Athena Award, an award given to women in business who mentor other women and strive for excellence in all they do. She looks forward to continuing learning, traveling, and meeting interesting people.

Kevin Hermening

Kevin Hermening is an active community volunteer, small business owner, and Marine veteran. He was the youngest of the Americans held hostage for 444 days at the US Embassy in Iran from 1979 to 1981, after Islamic terrorists captured the entire diplomatic staff. The hostages were captured after the Shah of Iran entered the US for medical care, and were freed on January 20, 1981, Inauguration Day in the US. Mr. Hermening often shares his experiences in captivity, the tragedy in the desert during the failed rescue mission, his views on Iran's present leadership, and the challenges the US faces in its dealings with Iran and the Middle East during presentations before students, civic organizations, business, military and church groups, and political audiences. His presentation, "Liberty & Leadership," provides a personal glimpse into a difficult time in our nation's history. He is a CERTIFIED FINANCIAL PLANNER™ and is the owner of Hermening Financial Group. Mr. Hermening served a total of 13 years in the Marine Corps and received an Honorable Discharge in 1994. He is the recipient of the US State Department's Award for Valor, and received the Prisoner of War Medal, and the Defense Meritorious Service Medal, the nation's highest peacetime military decoration, from the Department of Defense. Mr. Hermening challenges all Americans to remember daily the sacrifices that those who wear the uniform of their country make in service to our nation.

Recommended Book List

The fifth question that I asked during my interviews was "What is your favorite book?" Below is the list of their favorites.

"The Heart of The Sea" by Nathaniel Philbrick
recommended by Bart Starr Jr.

"Team of Rivals" by Doris Kearns Goodwin
recommended by Kevin Hermening

"The Rational Optimist" by Matt Ridley
recommended by Bart Starr Jr.

"The Better Angels of Our Nature"
by Steven Pinker
recommended by Bart Starr Jr.

"The Population Bomb" by Paul R. Ehrlich
recommended by Bart Starr Jr.

"The Bible"
recommended by Daniel Ally, Bart Starr Jr., and Kevin Hermening

"The Art of War" by Sun Tzu
recommended by Jim Frings

"Tale of Two Cities" by Charles Dickens
recommended by Richard Poirier

"The Road Less Traveled" by M. Scott Peck
recommended by Jay Forte

"The Laws of Success in 16 Lessons"
by Napoleon Hill
recommended by Tyrone M. Robinson III

"Life Changing Foods" by Anthony William
recommended by Susan Lang

"Little Bee" by Chris Cleave
recommended by Deidre Bradford

"Getting to Yes" by Roger Fisher and William Ury
recommended by Jim Frings

Acknowledgements

First and foremost, I would like to thank God for giving me the ability to believe in myself and big ideas. Without my faith, I would not be the person who I am today. Secondly, to my parents and family. Thank you for your unconditional love and support. This book would not be possible without you.

Thank you, Tyrone M. Robinson III, for inspiring me to write this book. Thank you, Jacob Bolanda, for your support and help. I cannot wait to watch you publish your book now!

Thank you to those who have given me their perspective and encouraged me to ask more questions. Your impact has been immeasurable. To those who have told me that questions are bad, and I should stop; thank you for making me want to ask more questions.

To my dearest friends who had no idea that I was writing this book, thank you for your patience and understanding when I needed time to work on "secret stuff."

Last, but certainly not least, to the people who took time out of their day to be interviewed. Your genuine thoughts, time, and responses are greatly valued.

Note: Other than the quotes attributed to specific people, all use of names, locations, and situations are hypothetical. Any other references to real people, locations, or situations are unintentional and should not be taken for fact.

About the Author

Christina Wenman is a 17-year-old high school student from Wisconsin who has a natural propensity to look at things from a different perspective. She is an extroverted-introvert, a practical dreamer, and a natural born entrepreneur. Other than spending this past year interviewing CEOs and motivational speakers, she is a typical teenager, involved in Student Senate, DECA, National Honor Society, FCCLA, Volleyball, and Softball. She is the youngest of four siblings and when she is not spending time with her family or hanging out with her friends, she is reading books, listening to TED talks, and preparing to study Business at a University in Wisconsin.

Made in the USA
Monee, IL
03 August 2021